BEETHOVEN

SONATA in C-Sharp Minor
Opus 27, No. 2 ("Moonlight")

Edited and Recorded by Robert Taub

To access companion recorded performances online, visit:
www.halleonard.com/mylibrary

Enter Code
4581-6226-6923-8133

On the cover:
Walk at Dusk
by Caspar David Friedrich
(ca. 1820)

© Christie's Images/CORBIS

ISBN 978-1-4234-2723-0

G. SCHIRMER, *Inc.*

DISTRIBUTED BY

HAL•LEONARD®
CORPORATION
7777 W. BLUEMOUND RD. P.O. BOX 13819 MILWAUKEE, WI 53213

www.schirmer.com
www.halleonard.com

CONTENTS

Sonata in C-sharp minor, Opus 27 No. 2 ("Moonlight")

Adagio sostenuto [♩ = 30 (♪ = 60)]

sempre pianissimo e senza sordini

Allegretto [♩. = 63]

p

Presto agitato [♩ = 88]

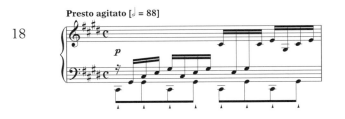

p

The price of this publication includes access to companion recorded performances online, for download or streaming, using the unique code found on the title page. Visit **www.halleonard.com/mylibrary** and enter the access code.

HISTORICAL NOTES

LUDWIG VAN BEETHOVEN (1770-1827)

THE PIANO SONATAS

In 1816, Beethoven wrote to his friend and admirer Carl Czerny: "You must forgive a composer who would rather hear his work just as he had written it, however beautifully you played it otherwise." Having lost patience with Czerny's excessive interpolations in the piano part of a performance of Beethoven's *Quintet for Piano and Winds*, Op. 16, Beethoven also addressed the envelope sarcastically to "Herr von Zerni, celebrated virtuoso." On all levels, Beethoven meant what he wrote.

As a composer who bridged the gulf between court and private patronage on one hand (the world of Bach, Handel, Haydn, and Mozart) and on the other hand earning a living based substantially on sales of printed works and/or public performances (the world of Brahms), Beethoven was one of the first composers to became almost obsessively concerned with the accuracy of his published scores. He often bemoaned the seeming unending streams of mistakes. "Fehler—fehler!—Sie sind selbst ein einziger Fehler" ("Mistakes—mistakes!—You yourselves are a unique mistake") he wrote to the august publishing firm of Breitkopf und Härtel in 1811.

It is not surprising, therefore, that toward the end of his life Beethoven twice (1822 and again in 1825) begged his publishers C.F. Peters and Schott to bring out a comprehensive complete edition of his works over which Beethoven himself would have editorial control, and would thus be able to ensure accuracy in all dimensions—notes, pedaling and fingering, expressive notations (dynamics, slurs), and articulations, and even movement headings. This never happened.

Beethoven was also obsessive about his musical sketches that he kept with him throughout his mature life. Desk sketchbooks, pocket sketchbooks: thousands of pages reveal his innermost compositional musings, his labored processes of creativity, the ideas that he abandoned, and the many others—often jumbled together—that he crafted through dint of extraordinary determination, single-minded purpose, and the inspiration of genius into works that endure all exigencies of time and place. In the autograph scores that Beethoven then sent on to publishers, further layers of the creative processes abound. But even these scores might not be the final word in a particular work; there are instances in which Beethoven made textual changes, additions, or deletions by way of letters to publishers, corrections to proofs, and/or post-publication changes to first editions.

We can appreciate the unique qualities of the Beethoven piano sonatas on many different levels. Beethoven's own relationship with these works was fundamentally different from his relationship to his works of other genres. The early sonatas served as vehicles for the young Beethoven as both composer and pianist forging his path in Vienna, the musical capital of Europe at that time. Throughout his compositional lifetime, even when he no longer performed publicly as a pianist, Beethoven used his 32 piano sonatas as crucibles for all manner of musical ideas, many of which he later re-crafted—often in a distilled or more rarefied manner—in the 16 string quartets and the nine symphonies.

The pianoforte was evolving at an enormous rate during the last years of the 18th century extending through first several decades of the 19th. As a leading pianist and musical figure of his day, Beethoven was in the vanguard of this technological development. He was not content to confine his often explosive playing to the smaller sonorous capabilities of the instruments he had on hand; similarly, his compositions demanded more from the pianofortes of the day—greater depth of sonority, more subtle levels of keyboard finesse and control, increased registral range. These sonatas themselves pushed forward further development and technical innovation from the piano manufacturers.

Motivating many of the sonatas are elements of extraordinary—even revolutionary—musical experimentation extending into domains of form, harmonic development, use of the instrument, and demands placed upon the performer, the piano, and the audience. However, the evolution of these works is not a simple straight line.

I believe that the usual chronological groupings of "early," "middle," and "late" are too superficial for Beethoven's piano sonatas. Since he composed more piano sonatas than substantial works of any other single genre (except songs) and the period of composition of the piano sonatas extends virtually throughout Beethoven's entire creative life, I prefer chronological groupings derived from more specific biographical and stylistic considerations. I delve into greater depth on this and other aspects of the Sonatas in my book *Playing the Beethoven Piano Sonatas* (Amadeus Press).

1795-1800: Sonatas Op. 2 no. 1, Op. 2 no. 2, Op. 2 no. 3, Op. 7, Op. 10 no. 1, Op. 10 no. 2, Op. 10 no. 3, Op. 13, Op. 14 no. 1, Op. 14 no. 2, Op. 22, Op. 49 no. 1, Op. 49 no. 2

1800-1802: Sonatas Op. 27 no. 1, Op. 27 no. 2, Op. 28, Op. 31 no. 1, Op. 31 no. 2, Op. 31 no. 3

1804: Sonatas Op. 53, Op. 54, Op. 57

1809: Sonatas Op. 78, Op. 79, Op. 81a

1816-1822: Sonatas Op. 90, Op. 101, Op. 106, Op. 109, Op. 110, Op. 111

From 1804 (post-Heiligenstadt) forward, there were no more multiple sonata opus numbers; each work was assigned its own opus. Beethoven no longer played in public, and his relationship with the sonatas changed subtly.

—*Robert Taub*

PERFORMANCE NOTES

For the preparation of this edition, I have consulted autograph scores, first editions, and sketchbooks whenever possible. (Complete autograph scores of only 12 of the piano sonatas—plus the autograph of only the first movement of Sonata Op. 81a—have survived.) I have also read Beethoven's letters with particular attention to his many remarks concerning performances of his day and the lists of specific changes/corrections that he sent to publishers. We all know—as did Beethoven—that musical notation is imperfect, but it is the closest representation that we have the artistic ideal of a composer. We strive to represent that ideal as thoroughly and accurately as possible.

General Observations

Tempo

My recording of this sonata is included in the published volume. I have also included my suggestions for tempo (metronome markings) at the beginning of each movement.

Fingering

I have added my own fingering suggestions, all of which are aimed at creating meaningful musical constructs. As a general guide, I believe in minimizing hand motions as much as possible, and therefore many of my fingering suggestions are based on the pianist's hands proceeding in a straight line as long as musically viable and physically practicable. I also believe that the pianist can develop senses of tactile feeling for specific musical patterns.

Pedaling

I have included Beethoven's pedal markings in this edition. These indications are integral parts of the musical fabric. However, since most often no pedal indication is offered, whenever necessary one should use the right pedal—sparingly and subtly—to help achieve legato playing as well as to enhance sonorities.

Ornamentation

My suggestions regarding ornamental turns concern the notion of keeping the contour smooth while providing an expressive musical gesture with an increased sense of forward direction. The actual starting note of a turn depends on the specific context: if it is preceded by the same note (as in Sonata Op. 10 no. 2, second movement, m. 42), then I would suggest that the turn is four notes, starting on the upper neighbor: upper neighbor, main note, lower neighbor, main note.

Sonata in F Major, Op. 10 no. 2:
second movement, m. 42

However, if the turn is preceded by another note (as in Sonata Op. 10 no. 2, first movement, m. 38), then the turn could be five notes in total, starting on the main note: main note, upper neighbor, main note, lower neighbor, main note.

Sonata in F Major, Op. 10 no. 2: first movement, m. 38

Whenever Beethoven included an afterbeat (Nachschlag) for a trill, I have included it as well. When he did not, I have not added any.

About the Edition

Footnotes within the musical score offer contextual explanations and alternatives based on earlier representations of the music (first editions, autograph scores) that Beethoven had seen and corrected. In specific cases that are visible only in the autograph score, I explain the reasons and context for my choices of musical representation. Other footnotes are intended to clarify ways of playing specific ornaments.

Above all, Beethoven's sonatas—as individual works, or taken together as a complete cycle—are pieces that we can listen to, learn, play, put away, re-learn, and perform again over and over—with only increasing joy, involvement, and meaning. For those of you looking at the musical score as you follow a recording, welcome. For those playing this piece for the first time, I invite you to become involved. And for those returning to this sonata after learning it previously—or comparing this edition to any other—I invite you to roll up your sleeves and start playing, for there is always more to do.

The expressive universe conjured up by the Beethoven piano sonatas is unprecedented, and unequalled.

Notes on the Sonata*

Sonata in C-sharp minor, Opus 27 no. 2 ("Moonlight") (1801)

First Movement: Adagio sostenuto

Imagine hearing the "Moonlight" Sonata for the first time. Striking is the character of the adagio first movement, its gently veiled sonorities shifting subtly, wisps of melodic fragments floating above. Most apparent to a pianist is the three-part texture: the underlying bass, the undulating accompaniment, and the sustained, legato top line. The alla breve time signature implies a pulse of two beats per measure, even within Beethoven's designation of Adagio sostenuto, which guards against the music's becoming lugubrious. The big question is how to use the pedal. At the beginning of the movement, Beethoven included two indications for *senza sordini* (without dampers): *Si deve suonare tutto questo pezzo delicatissimamente e senza sordini* and *sempre pianissimo e senza sordini* (this whole piece ought to be played with the utmost delicacy and without dampers; always very soft and without dampers). Do these guidelines mean to keep the

pedal down without changing it throughout the entire movement, or to use the pedal constantly but change it whenever necessary? I think the *senza sordini* indication is intended to create a special kind of sound—nothing dry, but sound bathed in its own warmth with hints of the surrounding harmonies. While I depress the pedal only slightly, just enough to raise the dampers off the strings to allow them to vibrate freely, the character of this movement requires the pedal to be changed discreetly to avoid creating harmonic sludge.

The *senza sordini* indications at the beginning of the movement, which are not followed by any *con sordini* indications, are fundamentally different from the *senza* and *con sordini* indications in the Largo of Beethoven's *Piano Concerto No. 3* or the pedal markings in Sonatas Op. 31 no. 2 ("Tempest") and Op. 53 ("Waldstein"), for these others have definite indications when the pedal should be depressed and when it should be lifted again. In Sonata Op. 27 no. 2 ("Moonlight"), *senza sordini* pertains to the entire first movement as a general approach to the quality of sound, similar to the initial *sempre pianissimo* indication.

It is this first movement for which the sonata is named, but not by Beethoven or even by his publisher. Ludwig Rellstab, a music critic, asserted that the mood of the first movement reminded him of the magic of the moonlight on Lake Lucerne.

The three-part texture that pervades this movement suggests different qualities of touch and sound for each different voice. The bass octaves are soft but deep, the undulating triplets are smooth and played with an accompaniment touch (flat, light fingers, not pressing too deeply into the keys), and the top line, although *pianissimo*, sings forth in a plaintive voice. In this Sonata *quasi una fantasia*, there is no second theme in the first movement—such were expectations stretched. The triplet accompaniment assumes a more melodic role and can be shaped accordingly as it is developed beginning in m. 32 on. Tension increases as new harmonies are explored, the bass remaining insistently on the G-sharp octave (the dominant) and the top line temporarily abandoned in favor of the searching qualities of the triplets.

In the short coda the portentous dotted rhythm is heard for the first time in the bass (but exclusively on G-sharps) as it exchanges registral placement with the triplets. The right-hand triplets come to the fore, however, in mm. 62-63

*Excerpted from *Playing the Beethoven Piano Sonatas* by Robert Taub
© 2002 by Robert Taub
Published by Amadeus Press
Used by permission.

when the crescendo-decrescendo markings are intended for the right-hand only. The situation is reversed in mm. 64-65 as the passage is repeated but with the crescendo and decrescendo markings now in the left hand. (Examination of the autograph score reveals that these crucial placements of the crescendo-decrescendo markings are, in fact, correct.) As the movement ends as quietly as it began, Beethoven wrote *Attaca subito il seguente*—an element of fantasia heard also in Op. 27 no. 1—and the second movement begins without any break in sound.

Second Movement: Allegretto

The point of connection between the first two movements is the enharmonic change from C-sharp minor of the first movement to D-flat major of the second. That is, the pitch of C-sharp is reinterpreted as D-flat, but now within a major harmony. For the performer this transformation takes place while the final C-sharp minor chord is still sounding within the fermata: the pianist's inner ear recasts the C-sharp as D-flat in preparation for delivering the surprise of the D-flat chord to the listener who in turn hears the transformation when this first chord is played. Despite the quicker pacing of the second movement, the mood is wistful and the textures delicate. The smooth lines of the Allegretto give way to *sforzando* syncopations in the trio, a contrasting spot of good humor in this sonata. I like to voice the left-hand chords in mm. 45-48 first to the tenor and then to the bass upon the repeat, giving a slight weight to the chromatic lines. Although the Allegretto ends with a rest, I would think it very much in keeping with quasi fantasia to begin the third movement almost right away. Once again, an enharmonic change (this time from D-flat Major back to C-sharp minor) is the pivot point.

Third Movement: Presto agitato

This last movement is the most extended of the three, and is the most overt dramatic center of the piece. I prefer a genuinely fast tempo; although the harmonic motion is not particularly rapid, finally the surface motion can be, and a feeling of agitation is generated from both speed and clarity. From the start a three-part texture analogous to that of the first movement is established: the bass line is distinct, the upwardly climbing 16th-note figures are a general middle area, and the top register is reached with the punctuated eighth-note chords, *sforzando*, staccato, in pedal.

Sonata in C-sharp minor, Op. 27 no. 2:
first movement, mm. 5-7

Sonata in C-sharp minor, Op. 27 no. 2:
third movement, mm. 1-2

The three-part texture (a, b, c) of the first movement is reestablished at the beginning of the third movement.

The tension in the music increases as the bass line descends chromatically from C-sharp to G-sharp (mm. 1-9), and intensity of touch can be increased by making both the left- and right-hand staccatos progressively sharper, especially with the melodic compression of mm. 7-9 and the concurrent crescendo.

Even during the melodic second theme (beginning in m. 21), I believe that the intensity level remains high and therefore use pedal only sparingly so that the left hand stays clear—and more concentrated and insistent than if it were blurred—as it accompanies the only "singing" line of the movement. Because of the intentionally discontinuous barring of the eighth-notes in m. 49 on, a breath of time can be taken so that the dialogue between the incisive *forte* and the songful *piano* measures is dynamically charged.

There are two fermatas, both over bare G-sharps, which is the dominant pitch and is hence fraught with expectations of resolution—one in m. 14 and the other in the parallel place in the recapitulation (m. 115). I hold these fermatas a long time. By creating feelings of suspense, seemingly spontaneously, they are crucial to the fantasia element, as is the four-measure cadenza-like passage in mm. 163-166, just four measures into the extended coda. There seems to be textual confusion about use of the pedal in these four measures (mm. 163-166). The first edition (Cappi, Vienna, 1802) has *con sord.* at the beginning of m. 163 (to countermand the *senza sord.* at the end of the previous measure), and *con sord.* again in m. 167. A *senza sord.* is missing. Plainly visible in the autograph, however, is this missing *senza sord*; it is in m. 165. Thus, although the first of these flourishes is meant to be played with "normal" pedaling, the second is more intense, plays a more forceful harmonic role, and hence is played with the dampers raised. Possibly because of the deletion of the *senza sord.* marking in the first edition, subsequent editions are inaccurate. Universal Edition has no pedal markings whatsoever for mm. 163-166, but the Peters Edition has pedal markings for both flourishes, not just the second. Henle has no pedal marking for the first flourish (m. 163) but has a pedal indication for the second (m. 165), thus following the autograph score; this approach make the most sense to me musically and seems the most expressive.

Although this sonata does not include a restatement of previous material (as did Sonata Op. 27 no. 1: the music of the Adagio was recalled at the end of the Allegro vivace), there is a subtle hint of the spirit of the first movement in the gradual meandering descent following the trill in m. 187. For this reminiscence in shaping of line and general texture, I allow the trill to slow down to the tempo of the eighth-notes so that they follow effortlessly. Although soft and slow, the adagio octaves in mm. 188-189 begin to gather tension again, with the G-sharp octave ever so slightly louder than the F-double-sharp octave as it resolves into the final part of the extended coda. At the very end, the three-part texture finally melds into one as the 16th-notes and cadential chords sweep up and down the entire range of the piano. The *forte* in m. 196 (G-sharp in the right hand), the *sforzando* in the following measure (E in both hands), and the *fortissimo* on the first C-sharp chord are all important; by successively spelling the triad of the home key (G-sharp, E, C-sharp) they subtly help create the air of finality. Thus, after the G-sharp *forte* I would drop slightly in dynamics to reach an even more intense *sforzando* on the Es played by both hands, saving the most sonorous level for the *fortissimo* C-sharp chords.

The first movement of this work may be among Beethoven's best-known piano compositions. But the complete sonata, particularly the anguished drama of the last movement, offers an artistic experience so many times fuller that I would urge anyone who has played only the first movement to become immersed in the rest of the work.

—*Robert Taub*

SONATA in C-Sharp Minor

Opus 27, No. 2

("Moonlight")

Dedicated to Countess Giulietta Guicciardi

Sonata in C-sharp minor
(Sonata quasi una Fantasia)
"Moonlight"

Ludwig van Beethoven
Opus 27 no. 2

Adagio sostenuto [♩ = 30 (♪ = 60)]

Si deve suonare tutto questo pezzo delicatissimamente e senza sordini.

sempre pianissimo e senza sordini*

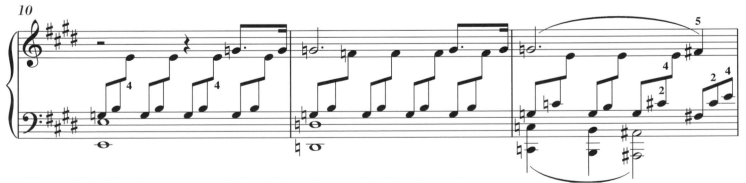

*The pedal indication (senza sordini—without dampers) is Beethoven's.

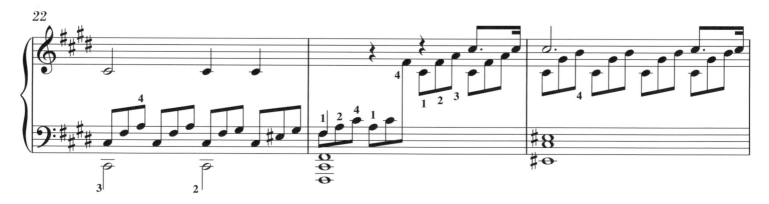

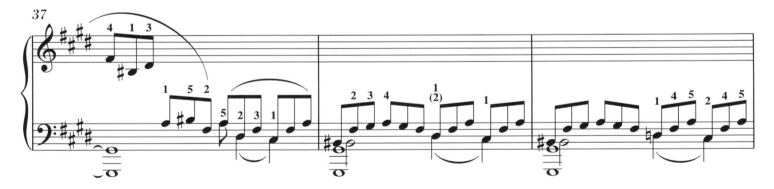

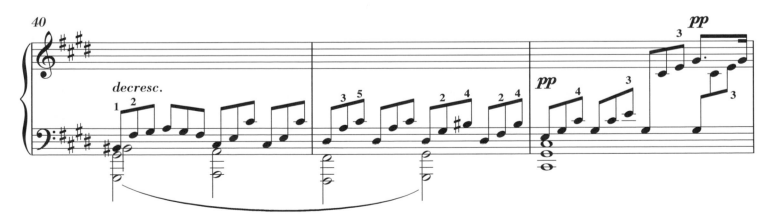

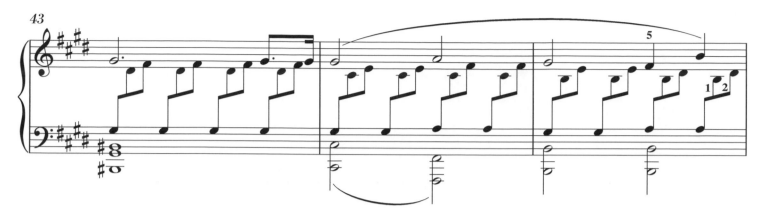

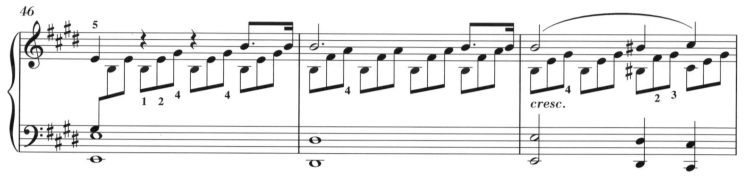

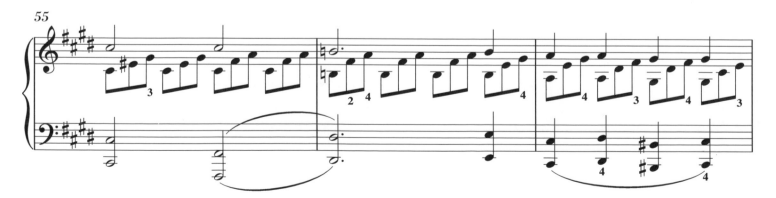

Attacca subito il seguente

Allegretto [♩.= 63]
La prima parte senza repetizione

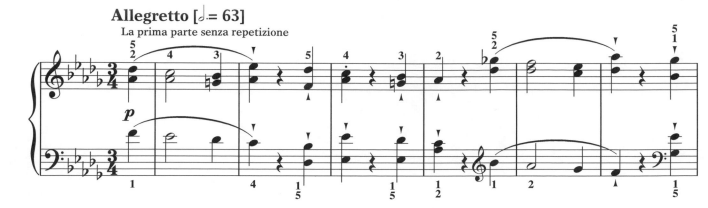

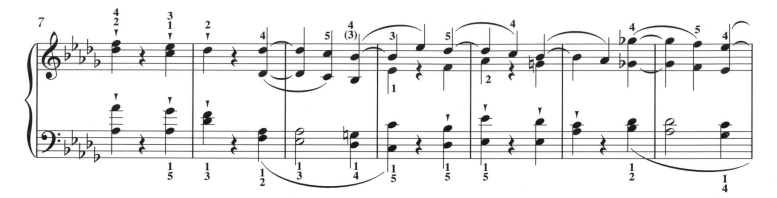

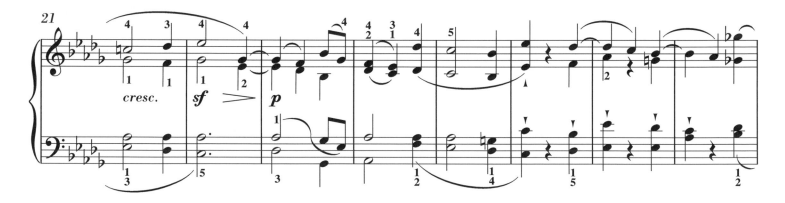

Fine

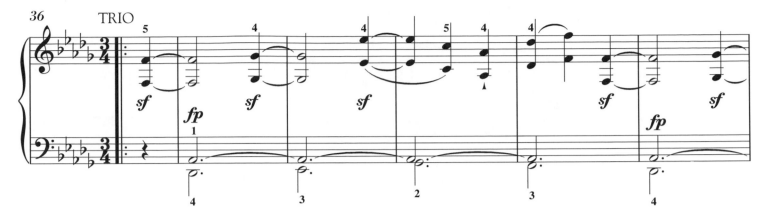

Presto agitato [♩ = 88]

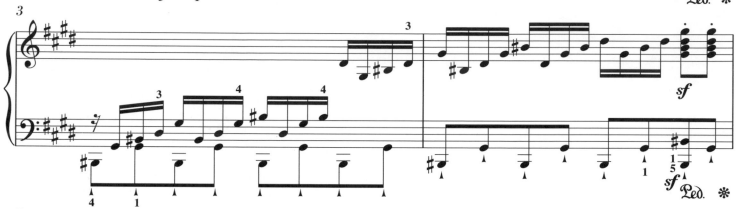

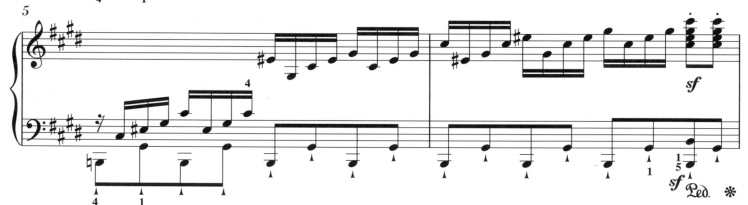

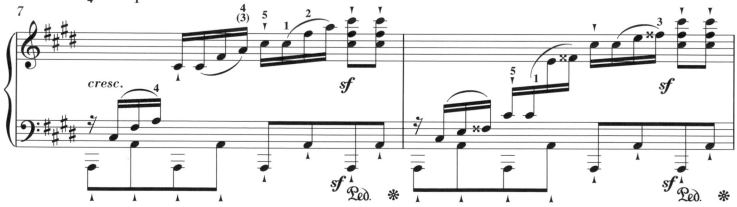

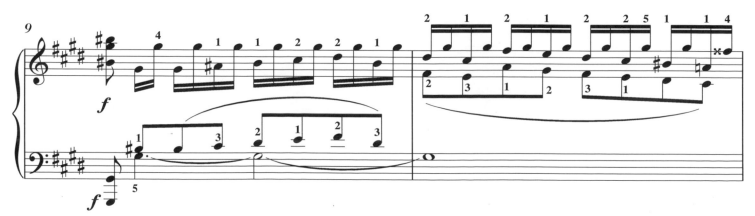

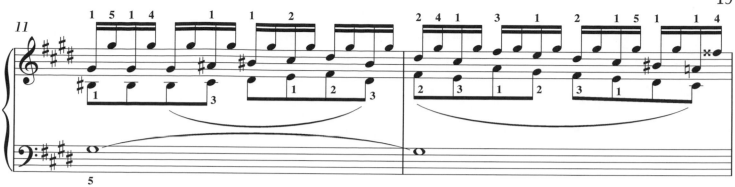

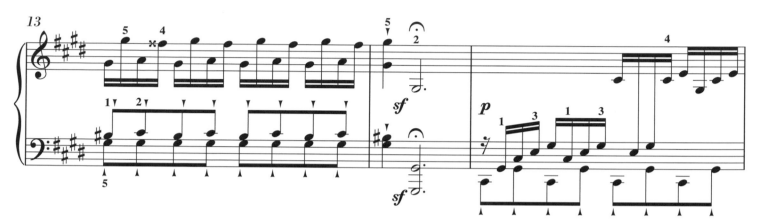

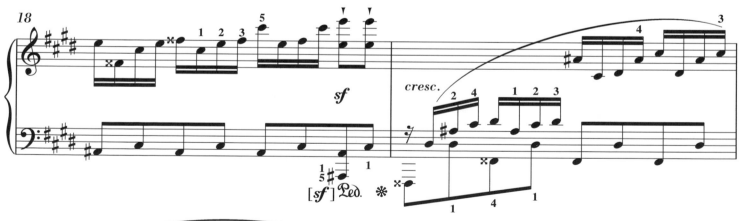

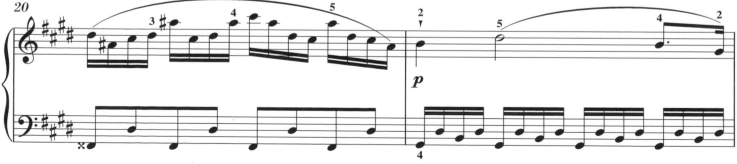

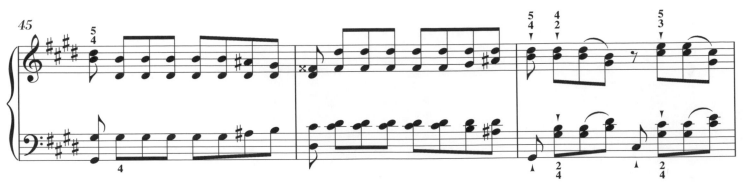

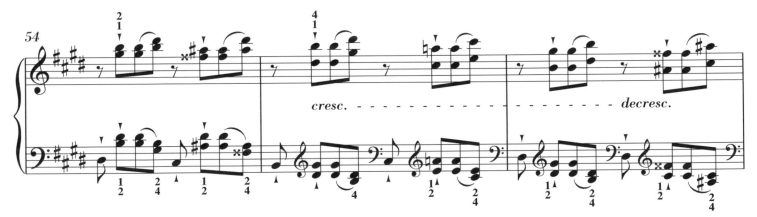

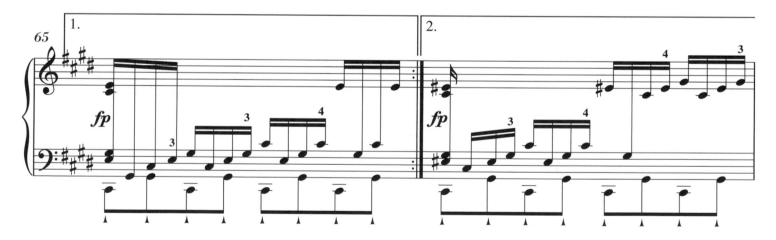

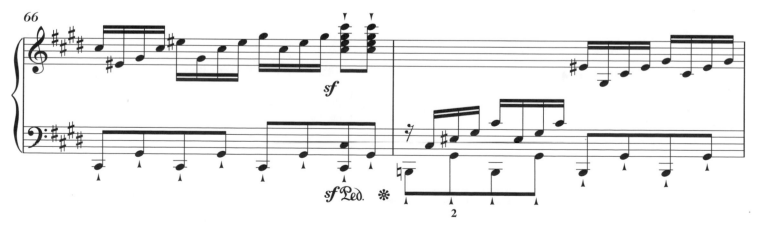

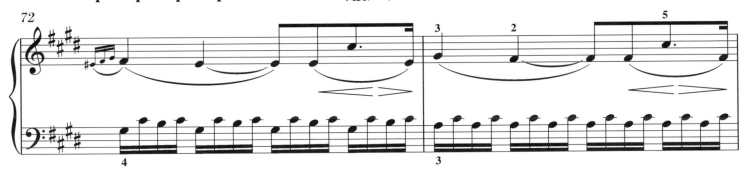

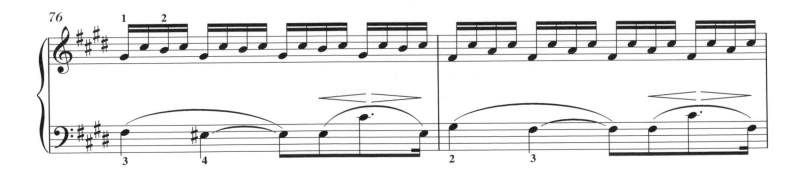

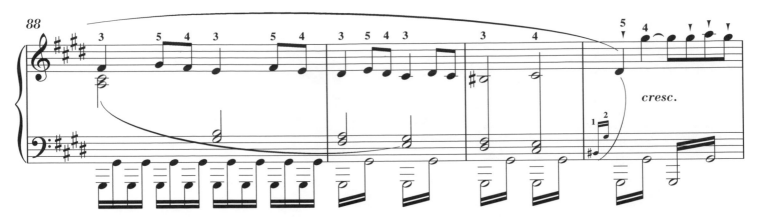

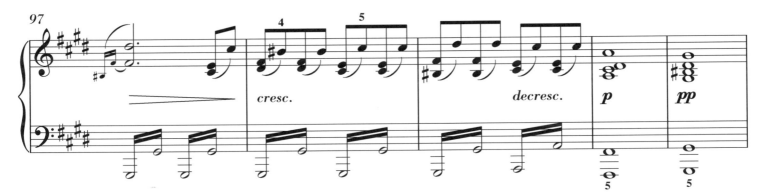

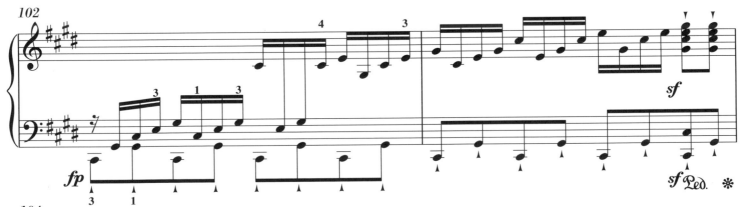

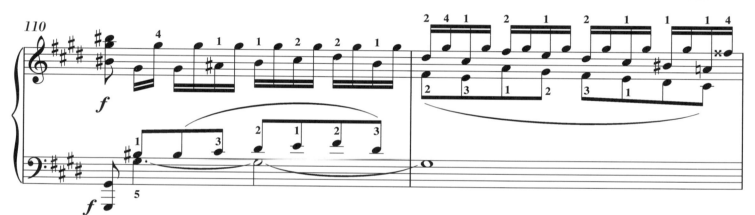

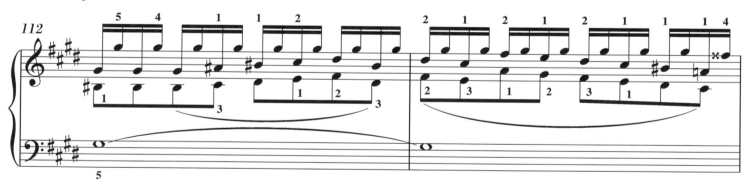

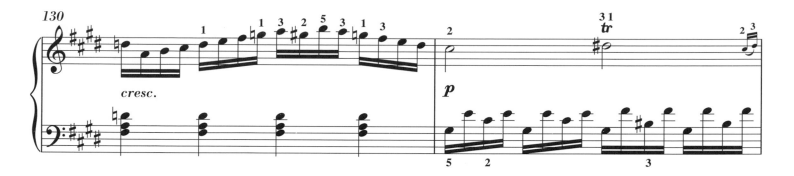

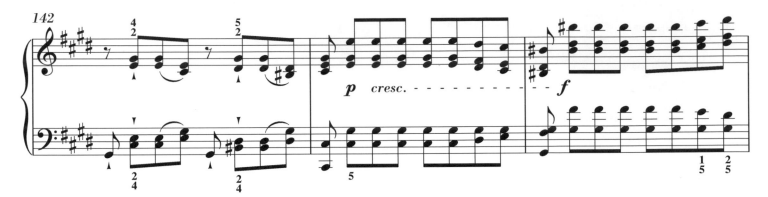

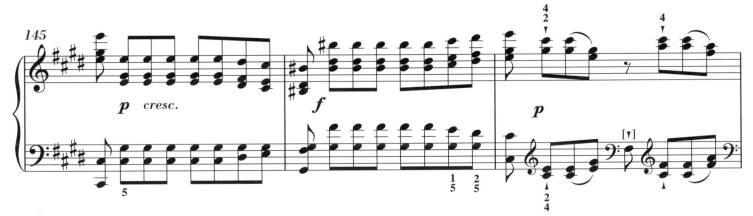

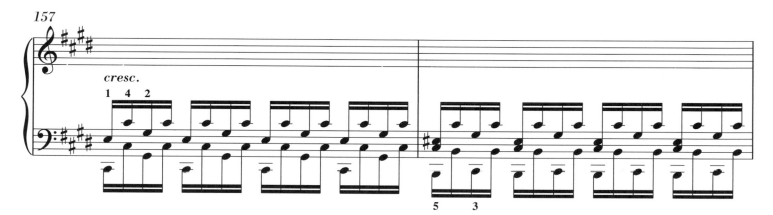

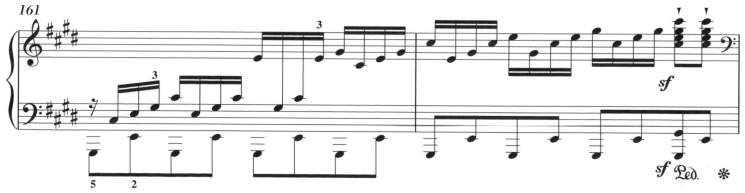

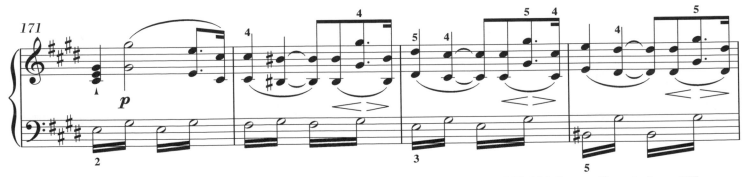

*As per Autograph score: "normal" pedaling in mm. 163–164; one long pedal in mm. 165–166; "normal" again in m. 167.

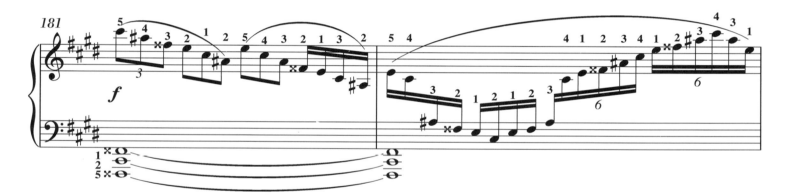

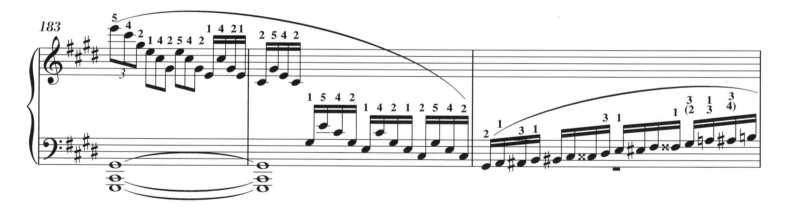

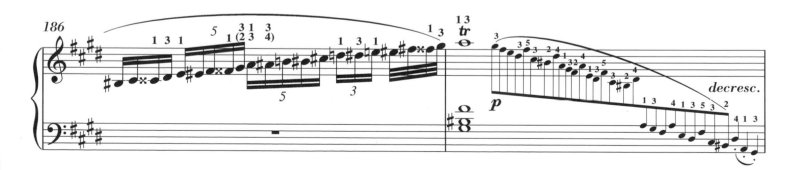

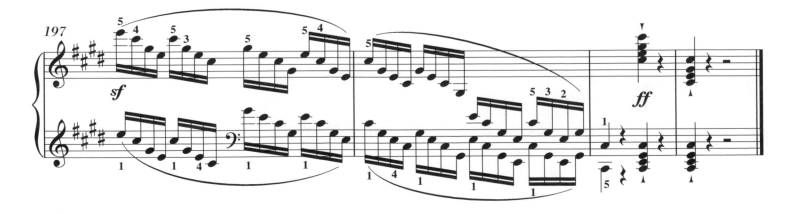

ABOUT THE EDITOR

ROBERT TAUB

From New York's Carnegie Hall to Hong Kong's Cultural Centre to Germany's *avant garde* Zentrum für Kunst und Medientechnologie, Robert Taub is acclaimed internationally. He has performed as soloist with the MET Orchestra in Carnegie Hall, the Boston Symphony Orchestra, BBC Philharmonic, The Philadelphia Orchestra, San Francisco Symphony, Los Angeles Philharmonic, Montreal Symphony, Munich Philharmonic, Orchestra of St. Luke's, Hong Kong Philharmonic, Singapore Symphony, and others.

Robert Taub has performed solo recitals on the Great Performers Series at New York's Lincoln Center and other major series worldwide. He has been featured in international festivals, including the Saratoga Festival, the Lichfield Festival in England, San Francisco's Midsummer Mozart Festival, the Geneva International Summer Festival, among others.

Following the conclusion of his highly celebrated New York series of Beethoven Piano Sonatas, Taub completed a sold-out Beethoven cycle in London at Hampton Court Palace. His recordings of the complete Beethoven Piano Sonatas have been praised throughout the world for their insight, freshness, and emotional involvement. In addition to performing, Robert Taub is an eloquent spokesman for music, giving frequent engaging and informal lectures and pre-concert talks. His book on Beethoven—*Playing the Beethoven Piano Sonatas*—has been published internationally by Amadeus Press.

Taub was featured in a 2003 PBS television program—*Big Ideas*—that highlighted him playing and discussing Beethoven Piano Sonatas. Filmed during his time as Artist-in-Residence at the Institute for Advanced Study, this program has been broadcast throughout the US on PBS affiliates.

Robert Taub's performances are frequently broadcast on radio networks around the world, including the NPR (Performance Today), Ireland's RTE, and Hong Kong's RTHK. He has also recorded the Sonatas of Scriabin and works of Beethoven, Schumann, Liszt, and Babbitt for Harmonia Mundi, several of which have been selected as "critic's favorites" by *Gramophone*, *Newsweek*, *The New York Times*, *The Washington Post*, *Ovation*, and *Fanfare*.

Robert Taub is involved with contemporary music as well as the established literature, premiering piano concertos by Milton Babbitt (MET Orchestra, James Levine) and Mel Powell (Los Angeles Philharmonic), and making the first recordings of the Persichetti Piano Concerto (Philadelphia Orchestra, Charles Dutoit) and Sessions Piano Concerto. He has premiered six works of Milton Babbitt (solo piano, chamber music, Second Piano Concerto). Taub has also collaborated with several 21st-century composers, including Jonathan Dawe (USA), David Bessell (UK), and Ludger Brümmer (Germany) performing their works in America and Europe.

Taub is a Phi Beta Kappa graduate of Princeton where he was a University Scholar. As a Danforth Fellow he completed his doctoral degree at The Juilliard School where he received the highest award in piano. Taub has served as Artist-in-Residence at Harvard University, at UC Davis, as well as at the Institute for Advanced Study. He has led music forums at Oxford and Cambridge Universities and The Juilliard School. Taub has also been Visiting Professor at Princeton University and at Kingston University (UK).